D1307707

COLOR CODES

Lynn M. Stone

Rourke
Publishing LLC
Vero Beach, Florida 32964

© 2009 Rourke Publishing LLC

All rights reserved. No part of this book may be reproduced or utilized in any form or by any means, electronic or mechanical including photocopying, recording, or by any information storage and retrieval system without permission in writing from the publisher.

www.rourkepublishing.com

PHOTO CREDITS: © Lynn Stone: cover, title page, 5, 6, 9, 11, 12, 13, 15, 16, 17, 18, 20, 21; © John Pitcher: page: 4; © Brian Opyd: page: 7; © Brad Phillips: page: 8; © Kitch Bain: page: 10; © Dmitry Deshevykh: page: 14; © Nicola Vernizzi: page: 15; © Jay Hess: page 19

Editor: Meg Greve

Cover design by: Nicola Stratford, bdpublishing.com

Interior design by: Renee Brady

Library of Congress Cataloging-in-Publication Data

Stone, Lynn M.

  Color codes / Lynn M. Stone.
     p. cm. -- (What animals wear)
  Includes index.
  ISBN 978-1-60472-307-6 (hardcover)
  ISBN 978-1-60472-785-2 (softcover)

  1. Animals--Color--Juvenile literature. 2. Protective coloration
(Biology)--Juvenile literature. I. Title.
  QL767.S86 2009
  591.47'2--dc22
                                              2008012967

Printed in the USA

CG/CG

R0429563663

Table of Contents

Color for Survival

The color of almost any animal helps it to survive. Color often helps an animal hide.

A hidden snake can catch small animals.

Colors That Camouflage

Most animals use their colors as **camouflage**. The animal's color or shape looks like whatever is around it.

Striped fur helps the tiger hide and allows it to sneak up on **prey**.

Small animals are often prey for bigger animals. Big animals may eat them if they do not hide.

The horned lizard hides by looking like the desert floor.

Colors That Signal

Some animal colors can show mood changes. They can also help animals find each other.

When a **mandrill** gets excited, its face becomes more colorful.

Seasonal Colors

Some animals change colors with the seasons. Their changing colors help them hide and hunt.

The short-tailed weasel has brown fur in summer and white fur in winter.

Several animals of the **Arctic** turn white in winter. The arctic fox and **ptarmigan** are among them.

This ptarmigan is changing from winter colors to summer colors.

Colors That Warn

Certain kinds of animals have bright colors to warn other animals to stay away.

South American tribes take poison from the colorful poison arrow frog and use it on their weapons.

Colors That Attract

Many birds turn bright colors during courtship. Feathers, eyes, and beaks may change colors.

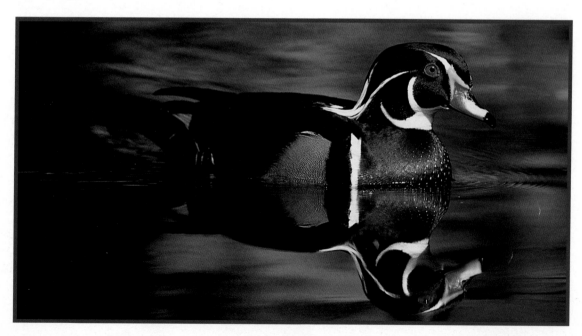

The bright feathers of a male wood duck help attract a **mate**.

Animal colors serve many purposes. All of them help animals survive.

A chameleon changes colors as its mood changes.

Glossary

 **Arctic** (ARK-tik): the cold region of the Earth's far north

 **camouflage** (KAM-uh-flahzh): to match closely to a surrounding in color or form

 **mandrill** (MAN-jril): a large baboon with a colorful face

mate (MATE): an animal's adult partner in raising a family

prey (PRAY): an animal that is killed and eaten by another animal

ptarmigan (TAR-mi-gin): a ground nesting bird of the north

Index

Further Reading

Jenkins, Steve. *Living Color*. Houghton Mifflin, 2007.

Petty, Kate. *Animal Camouflage and Defense*. Chelsea House, 2005.

Stockland, Patricia M. *Red Eyes or Blue Feathers: A Book about Animal Colors*. Coughlan, 2005.

Websites

www.brainpopjr.com/science/animals/camouflage/grownups.weml
www.geocities.com/EnchantedForest/Tower/1217/animal1.html
www.kidzone.ws/animals/index.html

About the Author

Lynn M. Stone is a widely-published wildlife and domestic animal photographer and the author of more than 500 children's books. His book *Box Turtles* was chosen as an Outstanding Science Trade Book and Selectors' Choice for 2008 by the Science Committee of the National Science Teachers' Association and the Children's Book Council.

24